IMAGES
of America

LIMESTONE

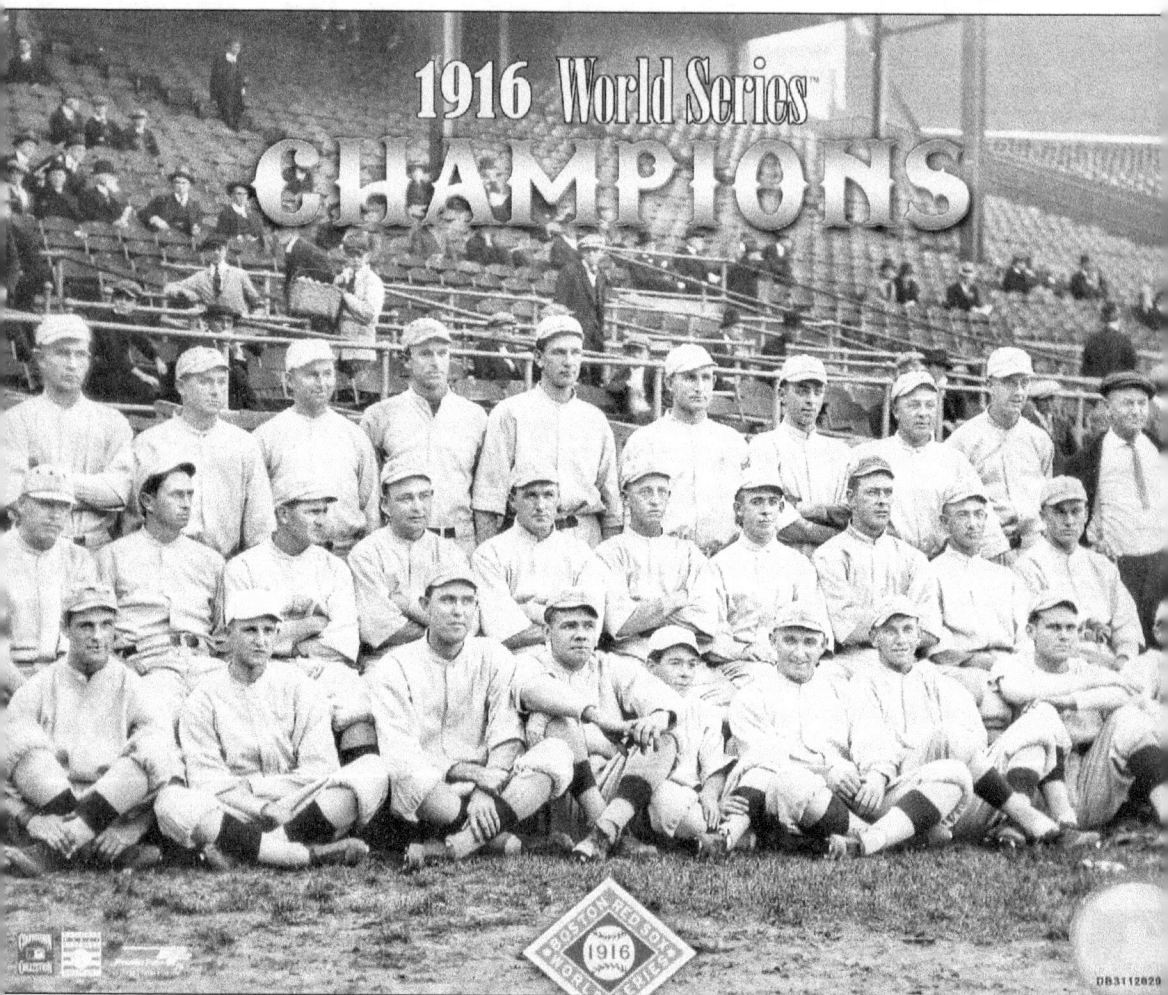

1916 World Series CHAMPIONS

The 1916 American League champions were the Boston Red Sox. Replacing Tris Speaker in center field that year was Clarence William "Tilly" Walker from Limestone and Washington College (second row, fifth from left). He went straight from schoolboy to the Washington Senators in 1911 and also played with the St. Louis Browns and the Philadelphia Athletics during an 11-year major-league career as an outfielder, with a career batting average of .281. Walker died in 1959 and is buried in Urbana Cemetery in Limestone.

ON THE COVER: Taken April 1, 1922, by an unknown photographer, this photograph shows the Limestone Motor Company, which sold Ford automobiles. It burned in 1939, and the blaze also destroyed the other wooden buildings at the southeast end of the business district. Among the people in the photograph (order uncertain) are dentist Dewey McCollum, Tex Farnsworth, owner John C. Smith (in the tie), Methodist preacher W. C. Harris, W. L. Broyles, and Charles Tagis. (Courtesy of Elva Tyree.)

IMAGES
of America

LIMESTONE

James Brooks

ARCADIA
PUBLISHING

Published by Arcadia Publishing
Charleston, South Carolina

Library of Congress Catalog Card Number: 2006924939

For all general information contact Arcadia Publishing at:
Telephone 843-853-2070
Fax 843-853-0044
E-mail sales@arcadiapublishing.com
For customer service and orders:
Toll-Free 1-888-313-2665

Visit us on the Internet at www.arcadiapublishing.com

To Janeth, who left her family in the Philippines to fly halfway around the world to be my wife and who makes every day more delightful than I could have imagined.

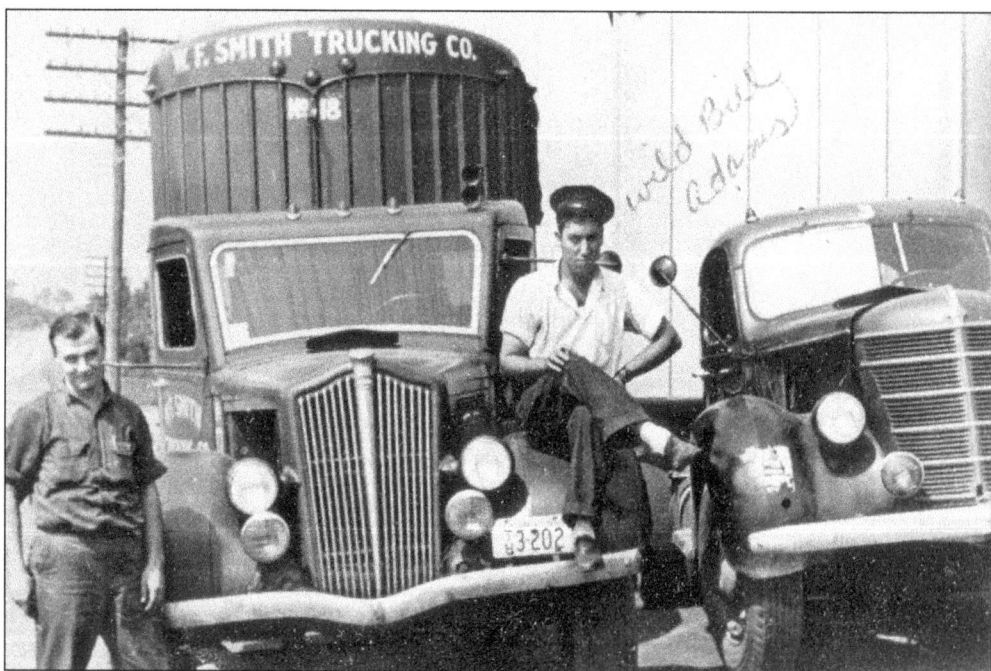

Truck No. 18 from W. F. Smith Trucking Company was driven by "Wild Bill" Adams (right) and Robert Fox in the late 1930s. Junior Samples of *Hee-Haw* television fame once drove for Smith. One time, he called collect from a small town in Georgia and said, "Billy, I've lost the truck." Through several collect calls, Smith directed Junior to backtrack one street at a time from the town square until he found his rig. The character portrayed on television wasn't acting; it was just Junior being himself.

CONTENTS

ACKNOWLEDGMENTS

It sometimes takes a tragedy to give a community the will to preserve its history. In Limestone's case, it was the death of Hugh M. Klepper, the last of his family to live in the 1792 Gillespie stone house, and the destruction of his prints and negatives. After years of taking photographs in and around Limestone, all but a few scattered images were lost in a single day of housecleaning by his heirs. That loss inspired others to take up the camera and use it to document their town. We are beholden to John A. Laws, who repaired watches and printed photographic postcards from an upstairs studio in the business district. Wilford "Bones" Broyles invested in a four-by-five Speedgraphic press camera and carried it on the front seat wherever he went. His daughter, Elva Tyree, saved the results of her father's work and made it available to me through two marathon scanning sessions. T. Claude Hensley used a single-lens reflex camera and close-up lenses to copy some photographs and take some originals. His encyclopedic memory of people and places filled in a lot of gaps. Hilda Pruitt was office manager of Davy Crockett Birthplace State Park. She preserved news clippings and documents and made her family album available. Dr. Earl Fletcher, president of Washington College Academy, made the archives available, and board member Martha Nell Estes spent an afternoon helping to pick out images. She is the daughter of W. F. Smith, and the next day, she opened up her family's history. Kathy Hensley and Bob Cutshaw also loaned extensive collections to be scanned. Mr. and Mrs. Kyle McQueen and artist Margaret Gregg have worked to preserve Broylesville and get it placed on the National Register of Historic Places. To these people and the others who shared their images, clippings, and personal stories, I give my heartfelt thanks.

To my editor at Arcadia Publishing, Maggie Tiller Bullwinkel, I am especially grateful for her gentle reminders and patience as I struggled to acquire competence with new digital photographic technology. A good editor walks a fine line to keep one mindful of deadlines while promptly providing assistance and encouragement. I have been fortunate indeed.

INTRODUCTION

In 1776, the North Carolina legislature formed Washington County, which was essentially the current state of Tennessee. In 1783, Greene County was formed, and for four years, the new state of Franklin had its state capitol in Greeneville.

The county line between Washington and Greene Counties basically follows Limestone Creek, a tributary of the Nolichucky River that gains its name from the many limestone outcrops on its banks and over which the creek flows.

Colonization followed the rivers, and in 1786, frontiersman David Crockett was born in a log cabin overlooking the Nolichucky River south of Limestone.

In 1780, the Reverend Samuel Doak founded Washington College, located midway between the county line and Jonesboro, the county seat that dates to 1779. Washington College was granted a charter as a college in 1791, the first such west of the mountains, although for much of its active life it was an academy, educating students through high school.

In 1792, mason Seth Smith built a limestone house in Limestone, and like many of the early brick and stone structures of the area, it was designed as a fortress to defend from Cherokee Indian attacks. It was used as a set for the filming of *Goodbye Miss Fourth of July* and was recently lovingly restored by Doug and Donna Ledbetter.

Limestone was originally called Freedom. After the arrival of the East Tennessee and Western Virginia Railroad in the 1850s, it was known as Klepper's Station. During the Civil War, it became the site of the Battle of Limestone Station as Union forces, pushed west from Knoxville, were met by a Confederate force led by Gen. Alfred E. "Mudwall" Jackson at Telford Depot east of Limestone on September 7, 1863. The 500 federals were pushed back to Limestone in a sharp engagement in which 60 were killed and 350 surrendered when they found retreat was cut off.

This prompted Lincoln's famous remark when informed that Burnside's advance was stalled outside Jonesboro. "Jonesboro, Jonesboro. Damn Jonesboro," the Great Emancipator said.

Jackson was a cousin of "Stonewall" Jackson who served as a quartermaster and was promoted to brigadier general. He took the field as needs required, and although ignored by history in this backwater of the war, his field record is distinguished.

Limestone prospered as a railroad town and was a shipping point for livestock trains. The pens adjoined Big Limestone Road, known as Main Street to everybody in town. W. F. Smith once received an entire train of Hereford cattle from Texas and drove them down the middle of the street to his feedlot.

At the end of the street stood the Lone Oak Hotel, where drummers (salesmen) would stay while renting a carriage from the livery stable to work country stores in Washington and Greene Counties.

Washington College, later Washington College Academy, served as high school for Limestone youth through a tuition agreement with the county. Limestone's most famous alumnus from a school that prides itself as a training ground for congressmen and ministers was a baseball player. Clarence Tilly Walker pitched and played right field for Washington College in 1909 and 1910.

He could throw a rock into Limestone Creek from his home atop the stone hill. He played 11 seasons in the major leagues, including the 1916 World Series. On his return to Limestone, Walker was the idol of local kids. He bought the needy ones shoes and overalls and took them all to ball games.

The town peaked as a trading center with the coming of Tennessee Highway 34 and the arrival of the automobile. Pendleton Smith opened the Farmers and Merchants Bank in the late 1800s. It still exists in the same location as BB&T. There was a Ford and Fordson Tractor dealership started by Pendleton's son, John C. Smith. The Lone Oak became a private residence in 1921 and has since passed out of the Broyles family.

The backbone of the community is the Ruritan Club, which formed the Limestone Volunteer Fire Department in 1957 with the purchase of a ladder/pumper truck from Pennsylvania, followed by a fire that destroyed the other end of Main Street.

Washington College reverted to academy status after educating several congressmen and other community leaders and long served as a private school that offered a superior education to children from rural families in Washington and Greene Counties. The unique feature of this school was that self-help students were required to work in the fields, vegetable gardens, and dairy barn as part of their tuition and in order to feed faculty, staff, and students with their own produce, meat, and dairy.

The school reached its peak when it served on a tuition contract with Washington County before David Crockett High School was built in the 1970s. In the decades since then, there have been several closings of the academy, the most recent three years ago. A re-opening is planned for 2006.

The nearby Washington College Ruritan formed a recycling center in order to clean up trash being dumped on roadsides. It is today a vital part of the county's solid waste disposal system and a model for recycling centers throughout the country. Funds from the sale of recyclables built the club's new brick clubhouse and sporting fields.

Through fire, floods, war, and economic downturn, this most isolated part of Washington and Greene Counties has hung together in a spirit that makes Limestone the bedrock community that it is. Lacking an incorporated municipal government, citizens band together in Ruritan clubs, churches, and coffee shops to solve the problems they daily face.

One

DAVY, DAVY CROCKETT

Frontiersman David Crockett was born in a log cabin on the bank of the Nolichucky River near Limestone in 1786. This lithograph by Chilts and Lehman in 1834 showed Crockett during the time he was in the U.S. Congress. Although he claimed to have had only a few days of schooling, his handwritten inscription is without error. He wrote, "I am happy to acknowledge the only correct likeness that has been taken of me."

"BE SURE YOU ARE RIGHT, THEN GO AHEAD."

W. A. NELSON, President.   H. C. REMINE, Vice-President.   Q. J. STOUT, Sec. & Treas.

—————————————THE—————————————

Davy Crockett Historical Society,

Cordially Solicits the Presence of Yourself and Friends at the

Celebration of the 103rd Anniversary of his Birth,

AT HIS BIRTHPLACE, NEAR

Limestone, East Tennessee, August 17th, 1889.

Preparations are being made to have the grandest demonstration ever held in East Tenn.

EXECUTIVE COMMITTEE.
A. E. GILLESPIE, Chairman.

J. J. SIMPSON,   JAKE BEWLEY,   N. B. REMINE,   E. L. WELLS.

This is an invitation from the Davy Crockett Historical Society announcing the 103rd anniversary of his birth on August 17, 1889. The Limestone Ruritan continued the birth celebration at the park for years until a dispute with park management led to separate celebrations held at the park and in town. The Ruritan event is currently a beauty contest.

David Crockett wrote on this 1834 painting by Asher B. Durand converted to a lithograph by New York printmaker Anthony DeRae: "I have this rule, for others when I am dead. Be always sure, you are right, then go, a head. David Crockett."

Gov. Frank G. Clement and Congressman B. Carroll Reece dedicated Davy Crockett Birthplace Park on August 17, 1958. The park sprang from the re-creation of Crockett's birthplace cabin (shown here) by the Limestone Ruritan and of a memorial with a stone contributed by every state in the union. The park today includes a small museum, swimming pool, and campground.

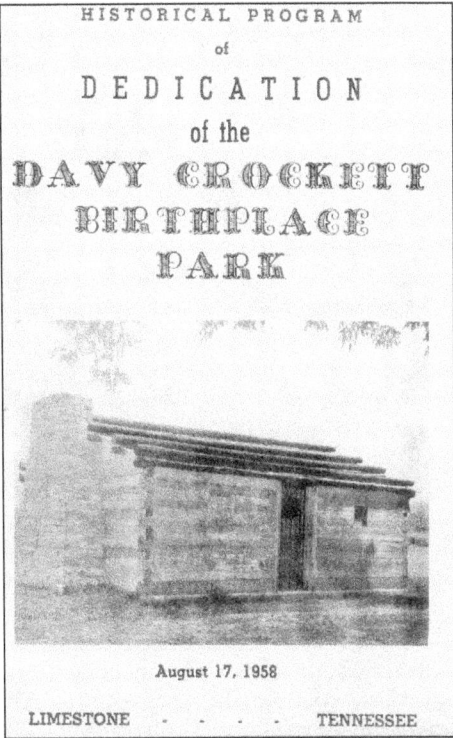

HISTORICAL PROGRAM
of
DEDICATION
of the
DAVY CROCKETT
BIRTHPLACE
PARK

August 17, 1958

LIMESTONE - - - - TENNESSEE

The Strong Springs Inn opened in 1880. It faced Limestone Creek shortly before it emptied into the Nolichucky River not far from the birthplace of David Crockett. The John Crockett family moved to Morristown when David was still in dresses, and the cabin site was later marked by a stone in the field. The inn included some wood from the original cabin. Builders Thomas Klepper and Tom A. Gillespie extolled the curative powers of the nearby spring waters. They envisioned vacationers debarking from the train in Limestone and making a carriage ride down the creek to the inn.

—Bound for Strong Spri—

This early-20th-century photograph is captioned, "Bound for Strong Springs." It was a Limestone School class outing. The spa on the grounds of what is now Davy Crockett Birthplace State Park was originally the site of a mill owned by Bill Collet. The hotel displayed some Crockett artifacts including a stone Native American ax used in the wars. Following a shooting at the hotel in 1912, it was decided that the waters had lost their curative powers, and the inn was closed. It remained for years after as a private house, with interior walls papered with newspapers. It was torn down by the state when it was decided it lacked historic merit.

Roscoe Stonecipher farmed on the present site of Davy Crockett Park. From left to right, Sarah Stonecipher Bayless, Lena Remine, and Macie Stonecipher are shown here on a visit to the old home place in 1940.

Two

It Takes a Village

Baby Mary Alice McCracken was posed in the lap of her sister, Judy, in a chair in the middle of Main Street with little fear of being run over by an automobile. The photograph was taken after the flood of 1921 swept away the board sidewalks. The street is paved, but the unbroken facade of wooden buildings is intact, so it was taken before the northeast end of the street burned in 1957.

Limestone kept most of its Wild West facade on Big Limestone Road, which everybody calls Main Street, until it burned in 1957. These girls stopped for a Coke and some after-school candy in the early 1950s. Did they see the similarity between their downtown, with its false-front buildings, and those in the movies?

John C. Smith was almost never without his cigar. The Farmers and Merchants Bank was founded by his father, Pendleton Smith. John C. owned the Limestone Motor Company, and when it burned, he built Keebler-Smith Hardware in its location. He later entered businesses with his son, W. F. Smith, at Smith Grain (trucking) and Smith-Dale Farms (Hereford cattle breeding).

Nell Shields Smith, wife of John C. Smith, was known to everyone as "Mur" because her children couldn't pronounce "mother."

The Big Burley Tobacco Warehouse in Johnson City was managed by John C. Smith (second row, fifth from left) when this crop was brought in by his fellow Limestoner Walter "Jeff" Martin (second row, third from left). Other farmers from Limestone are Freddy Squibb and Joe Painter (first row, fourth and fifth from left), Ray Houser (second row, far right); and Lyle Broyles (alone in the third row with baseball cap). (Photograph by A. B. Foster.)

In small towns, everybody has a nickname. This is Eugene Shields "Bucky" Smith, W. F. "Billy" Smith's brother.

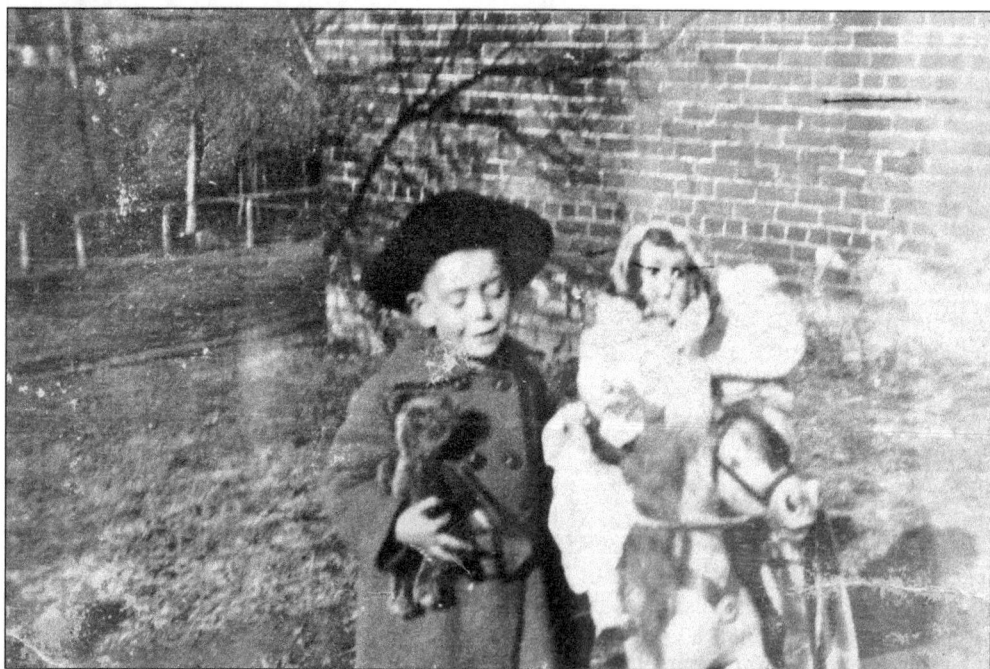

W. F. "Billy" Smith was a smooth talker in his teddy bear days and improved with age.

Billy Smith is shown on his return home on leave from military school. He attended the Baylor School in Chattanooga.

Jack Chambers Smith is shown dressed as an Elizabethton cheerleader when she was dating Billy Smith in the 1930s. What girl could resist a convertible?

17

Jack Chambers Smith looked pensive in her engagement photograph.

Martha Nell and her sister, Joan Clark Smith (from left to right, first row), were photographed at a family occasion in 1944. From left to right in the second row are John C. Smith, Meda Farnsworth, Bobby Smith, and Billy Smith. They are in front of John C.'s house in Limestone. Built of brick fired by slaves on the spot, the house is said to have been a hospital during the 1863 Battle of Limestone Station, and casualties are supposed to be buried under the porch.

At age 10, Martha Nell Smith claimed she met every governor of Tennessee but the one in jail. As teenagers, she and sister, Joan, went on to pose as cover girls for the *Hereford Journal*. She taught for 38 years in five states, retiring in 2006. She has been on the board of Washington College Academy since Paul Gabinet was president and saw the school revive from two closings.

Maxie Clark Smith, daughter of John C. and Nell, died at age 23 in 1941 of tuberculosis, two years after this photograph was taken.

W. F. Smith and his wife, Jack, pose in front of their car at the beginning of his career in the 1930s.

This photograph of W. F. Smith was taken on June 22, 1975. He started a trucking company in the 1930s that grew to 100 trucks and 250 employees, hauling perishables, grain, and livestock throughout the southeast. Runs were made with two drivers if perishable produce was involved. Smith was also a Hereford cattle breeder and shipped entire trainloads into and out of Limestone. He went bankrupt on the commodities market, moved away from Limestone, and died at the age of 59.

John C. Smith found himself "in the doghouse" on a Myrtle Beach vacation.

The Smith family vacationed in Myrtle Beach, South Carolina, in the 1950s. From left to right are Nell Shields Smith, Martha Nell Smith, Anna Shields Mitchell (mother of Johnny Mitchell), and Joan Smith McQueen.

Johnny "Packin'" Mitchell worked for Western Union in 1939. He worked construction, drove a convertible, and left a trail of broken hearts in Limestone. He learned about fighting chickens from his father and became internationally famous for his Johnny Mitchell Reds, which sell today for $1,000 apiece. During World War II, he fought on Guadalcanal and Luzon in the Philippines, and landed at Nagasaki, Japan, after the nuclear blast. He later served on the Washington County Commission and was a county purchasing agent.

Johnny Mitchell (right) is pictured at the Tri-Cities Airport with Junior Bodina from Davao, Philippines, one of the top gamecock fighters on Mindanao, where it is a legal sport. Mitchell is a living legend there ever since his first rooster won 12 fights in a row. Mitchell's opponents on the county commission once steered newspaper photographers to his chicken house shortly before the election. "I got more votes that year than anybody," Mitchell said.

This unidentified Limestone lady on horseback with a rifle reflects the rugged frontier spirit of the community.

The Lone Oak Hotel was built in the 1880s. In the days when the railroad was the only way into town other than dirt roads, it did a brisk business with railroad crews and salesmen working country stores by horse and buggy rented from the livery stable. It was purchased in 1921 by Wassan and Leora Broyles. Although they sometimes rented out rooms in the 14-room structure, it has remained a private home since then.

Thomas Jefferson Farnsworth and his wife, Finette, (seated) were the parents of David Hunter Farnsworth and Leora Farnsworth Broyles.

Wassan and Leora Broyles pose with their young family. From left to right are (first row) Winfred "Toddy," baby W. T., and Leora; (second row) Marion Lee, Wassan, and Gilford "Bones" Broyles.

Joe Broyles was a mechanic for Smith Grain and had an endless interest in tinkering. One of his inventions, the air bicycle, is still in Wassan Broyles's garage in downtown Limestone.

Gilford "Bones" Broyles's photographs of Limestone in the 1930s and 1940s preserve the town and its people for future generations. He carried a four-by-five Speedgraphic camera while working as a wrecker driver for Broyles Garage and often sold wreck photographs to the newspaper.

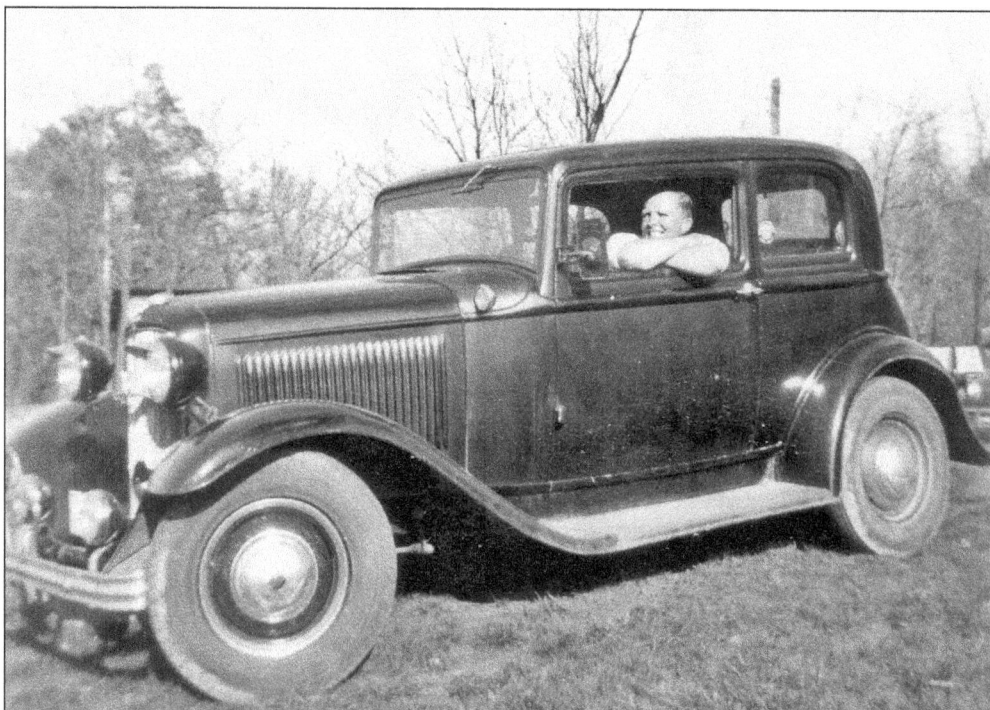

Winfred "Toddy" Broyles, like most young men, was proud of his car. He worked as a clerk at Keebler-Smith Hardware most of his life and lived in a room under the business. He never married.

W. T. Broyles shows agility while working on a wire across Main Street. The Broyles family is known for mechanical ability, inventiveness, curiosity about how things work, and a wry sense of humor. Today W. T., at 85, is the oldest active private pilot at the Greeneville–Greene County Airport. People in Limestone come out to wave when he flies over in his Cessna 172, and he prefers to land in the grass beside the runway, which he announces on the radio as landing on Runway 23A.

Leora "Mamaw" Broyles greets guests at a family reunion at the Lone Oak Hotel. She is in the center, facing the camera.

Leora Bell Farnsworth (left) poses with her cousin Florence Seaton early in the 20th century. She was soon to marry Wassan Broyles.

"Gilford took this when I was getting ready for bed," Leora "Granny" Broyles wrote on the back of this photograph.

Johnny "Butch" Broyles was a driver for General Deaver in Washington, D.C. His wife was a secretary who once rode with Pres. Ronald Reagan on Air Force One. As a grandson of Wassan and Leora Broyles, he represents the next generation of a family whose contributions to Limestone are so numerous that the various Broyles Streets in town need first names.

D. W. (left) and Phebe Remine are shown at home. He came to Greene County in 1847 from Virginia.

D. W. and Phebe Remine had 14 children. Some of them are shown here with their parents from left to right: (first row) Maynard, Phebe, D. W., Fred; (second row) Minnie, Tot, Kate, Cal, Bertie, Annie, and Schyler.

Alfred "Bub" Gillespie, a member of Limestone's small black community, is shown in the 1930s on his way home from the store.

Bill Garrison the barber mugs for the camera. He was said to be one of the best-looking men in town, but you would never know it from this photograph.

Bob Mausolph was cast as the station master in the television movie *Goodbye Miss Fourth of July*. In this shot taken at the railway station in nearby Chuckey, he is with Louis Gossett Jr. Several scenes were shot at the Gillespie stone house in Limestone, home to the film's Janus family, played by Chris Sarandon, Chantal Contouri, and Roxanna Zal.

The Limestone bus to Kingsport was replaced in 1947 by this new model, with Elmer Hensley the driver. The arrival of new auto styling, beginning with the 1949 Ford, combined with good economic times, spelled doom for the bus line.

The Gillespie-Klepper stone house is Limestone's oldest. It was built in 1792 by Seth Smith, who built four structures in Washington County, three of which are still standing. Col. George Gillespie and his son, Tom, were pioneer settlers of Tennessee. Colonel Gillespie was one of the leaders of the Overmountain Men who defeated Maj. Patrick Ferguson at the Battle of King's Mountain (1780), the turning point of the Revolutionary War. The house passed to the Klepper family, relatives of the Gillespies. This photograph showing one of the Kleppers was taken c. 1880, when the house still had a shake shingle roof. In those days, the community was known as Klepper's Station. The house was vacant and went through a period of decay after the death of H. M. Klepper in 1975.

A father's pride in his son and namesake is evident on the face of Will T. Cannon as he holds William T. Cannon Jr., *c.* 1920s.

Claude Hensley and Imogene Holland are pictured in front of the Ben Fox chicken house in 1958. At six-feet-three-inches tall, Hensley usually played center or forward for Washington College's basketball team.

Whether it's politics, crops, or weather, the discussions continued at Limestone Hardware in the days before people were entertained by television. To call this store a hardware store was like calling Wal-Mart a clothing store. They sold everything.

The late Paul Campbell is pictured in front of his home, the former Bethesda Academy, an orphanage and trade school next to Urbana Cemetery where the *Rural Searchlight* may have been printed between 1905 and 1908. The academy employed six men and women for a payroll of $135 a month, but a typhoid outbreak and financial problems closed it.

Richard Donoho solders a church window. He and his wife, Freda, have a studio, Artistry in Glass, that is today the most active business in downtown Limestone other than the bank.

Bob Cutshaw ran the grocery store in Limestone for his wife, Maude, who owned it, from 1984 to 1999, after previous owners George and Sandra Jaynes moved into country government. Cutshaw continues as secretary for the Limestone Volunteer Fire Department.

Three

A Walk Downtown

Martha Nell, one of W. F. Smith's daughters, is pictured on Main Street prior to 1957. In 2006, she retired from a 38-year teaching career in five states that included Westview School, and she is currently on the board at Washington College Academy.

A girl, believed to be Margaret Hall, walks past the Ben Fox chicken house and the O. G. Yeager store on the northeast end of Main Street.

The Fox and Walker Livery Stable c. 1890 was located on the end of Main Street. Those identified include Bob Fox (standing holding bridal), Alex Williams (astride horse), and Bart Sheppard (back far right). Behind is the home owned by undertaker W. N. Walker, father of baseball player Clarence Tilly Walker.

The W. O. Anderson residence on this rock hill was the home of former Boston Red Sox center fielder Clarence Tilly Walker. Walker often entertained his fellow major leaguers here. According to local legend, Babe Ruth, Walker's old Red Sox teammate, was a guest in the home. After his baseball career, Walker went to work for the Tennessee Highway Patrol. He is remembered as a man who loved children. He sometimes treated a group of local kids to a Johnson City Cardinals minor league baseball game, and he always had a stick of Beech Nut gum handy for a young fan. The house burned in the 1960s when it was owned by W. J. Probst.

Tilly Walker and his father moved to this house on Maple Street after selling the old Victorian house on the rock hill, and Tilly lived here until shortly before his death in 1959. He is buried at Urbana Cemetery in Limestone.

An unidentified group of people stands in front of the Thompson General Merchandise Store, *c*. 1918.

Fashionable young people pose on the railroad track in Limestone. The *c*. 1918 photograph is one of the few from the Hugh M. Klepper collection that survived after his death in 1975. Seated beside the track from left to right are two unidentified, Lucy Richardson, Hugh Klepper, and ? Stalopes.

The Gillespie-Klepper house was vacant and deteriorated after the death of Hugh M. Klepper. It was lovingly restored by Doug and Donna Ledbetter, including a new roof and rafters. Except for a modern kitchen and family room added to the back, it is close to the way it was in Col. George Gillespie's time, except for plumbing and subdued electric lighting.

William J. Strain was Limestone's first postmaster, and his home on Opie Arnold Road was believed to be the original post office until he built the downtown post office and store. He also built the Lone Oak Hotel around 1880. He was married to Synthia Broyles, and they had three children. This home is now owned by Greg and Sandy Lyon.

From left to right, Schuyler Remine, Agnes Remine, and Agnes Starrit came into town and pulled up in front of Limestone Motor Company to demonstrate that the old reliable team and wagon would never be replaced by those newfangled motorcars.

Before the facade was painted up as a Ford dealership in the 1920s, the Limestone Motor Company looked like this. T. Claude Hensley lived over the hill outside of town the night this automobile dealership and the entire business district up to the vacant lot by the bank burned. He remembers the red glow in the sky and hearing shotgun shells exploding in the stores.

On the left is Jaynes and Company. The post office is on the right. Postmaster J. H. Tipton, in the doorway, also endorsed the opening of the Bethesda Orphanage in 1908 and was on the board of directors. The space between the two buildings was later covered with false doors to conceal a coal shed.

The Limestone tomato cannery stood at Main Street and River Street in 1925. When photographs were taken, everybody came out and even stood on the roof. The cannery later burned.

The Limestone Roller Mill was run by J. H. Kirby *c.* 1905 but is known by most residents living today as the old Williams Mill. This gristmill burned in the 1940s.

The Nolichucky warehouse at the end of Maple Street was the main shipping point for produce and tobacco from the region. Around the turn of the 20th century, Limestone was a bigger railway shipping point than Jonesborough, the county seat.

This view looks east on Main Street around the turn of the 20th century from a postcard believed to have been made by John A. Laws. The first three buildings on the left burned in the 1939 fire. The bank survived the blaze. The next wooden building is the Max Finkel general merchandise store. Note the tree trunk on the right side of the dirt street. East Tennessee was primarily a source of iron ore and forestry products at this time.

JOHN A. LAWS,
Jeweler Photographer,
——AND DEALER IN——
WATCHES AND CLOCKS
Repairer of Sewing Machines and all kinds of Jewelry.
SATISFACTION GUARANTEED.

John A. Laws is believed to be the photographer who made the early photographic postcards of Limestone. Working from an upstairs studio, his card proclaims that he is a jeweler and photographer who also repaired watches, clocks, and sewing machines. He liked to pose individuals standing apart from one another. In the case of the cannery photograph, he spaced people on the roof like lightning rods.

This view of Main Street Limestone between 1905 and 1920 shows raised board sidewalks. They were necessary because Limestone Creek, behind the commercial block, regularly spilled over its banks. The Coca-Cola sign on the nearest building dates the photograph, believed to have been made by John A. Laws.

Leroy Bailey (left) and Hershel J. Barlow in front of Hartman's Produce wait for a break in traffic so they can cross the street.

Father and son, Teddy (left) and Frank Williams, take a stroll downtown. Frank played center for the Limestone grammar school basketball team. He was a free spirit who was unable to adapt to the discipline imposed by Roy "Pop" Mullins at Washington College. He returned to Limestone to retire after spending most of his working life in DeKalb, Illinois.

The Limestone Bank is seen over the W. F. Smith cattle pens with the Max Finkel store at top, c. 1948. The 1957 fire claimed the latter two frame buildings. The privy behind the bank functioned as the city restroom.

The Esso station on State Route 34 on the west end of town was the place for men to hang out. From left to right are Bob Ginispie, one of Limestone's small African American community, unidentified, Sam McCall, unidentified, Red Hartman, and two unidentified discussing the weather, crops, or yesterday's card game in the honeysuckle behind the station.

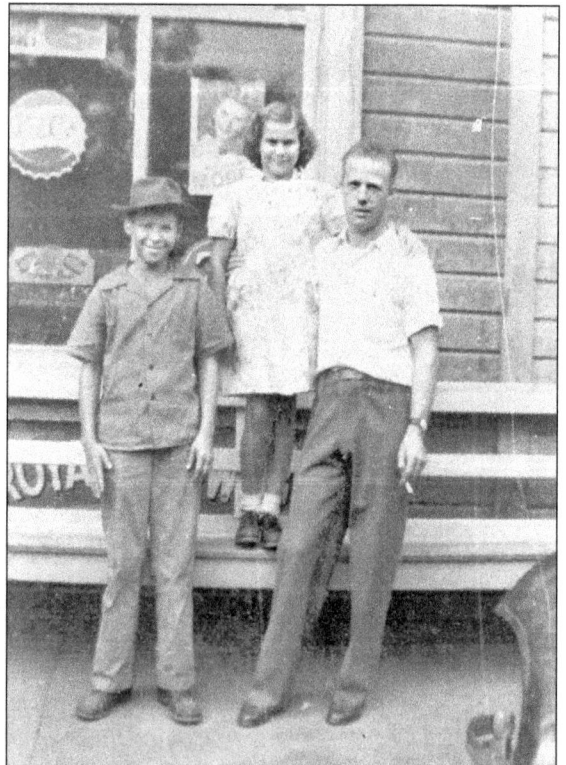

The Finkel store housed businesses run by several merchants over the years. Between 1946 and 1948, it was a pool hall run by Murphy Riddle (right). With him in this photograph are Glen (left) and Wilma Hensley.

During World War II, it wasn't unusual to empty out the restaurant and put everybody squinting into the sunshine for a photograph to send to a local soldier overseas. The guys on the loafer's bench didn't need to do a thing.

Winfred "Toddy" Broyles (behind counter) and Raymond Holt negotiate a purchase at Limestone Hardware. It couldn't boast of neat displays or of the store being cozy warm in winter, but most customer requests were greeted with, "I've got it, if I can find it." Toddy was a clerk at the store much of his life.

Wintertime meant a rook tournament at Velma Saylor's store downtown. With two tables going at once, the action probably went on for hours. In the early 1950s, television hadn't yet made inroads into small town social gatherings. Note the boxes of Fab, Lux, Dreft, and other soaps.

This view shows Limestone in winter 1947, with the old Finkel store and a Coca-Cola sign. From left to right, the next two-story building is the Masonic Lodge, followed by Bill Garrison's barber shop. The Southern Railway depot is at right. In the background, on the other side of Limestone Creek, is the spire of the Limestone Methodist Episcopal Church.

The Ben Fox chicken house at the end of Main Street was a favorite place to put up circus posters. Fox purchased chickens and eggs from area farmers and shipped them out by truck every few days. The two men are unidentified.

The loafer's bench downtown sometimes got a workout in the 1950s. From left to right, unidentified, S. B. Stanton, unidentified, Ben Fox, and T. E. Alexander discuss the crop outlook while waiting their turns at Bill Garrison's barbershop.

The Anderson Café was known as the east end service station, no matter who owned it over the years. As State Route 34 dropped down the hill into Limestone, it made a sharp bend around the Anderson Café, run by Paul and Zelda Anderson. Up until recent years, there were four or five places in town to buy gasoline. Now the nearest spot is out on the U.S. Highway 11E bypass, about two miles from downtown. The Anderson Café was torn down to make room for the current Limestone Volunteer Fire Department station.

Yeager's Esso stood on State Route 34 at the southwest end of town, just before the road turned under the Southern Railway. Hilda Pruitt remembered as a young girl impulsively using the punch board and winning a box of candy. Her father was angry because he then had to pay a quarter to support her gambling habit.

Yeager's Esso station was owned by Hugh M. Klepper, who lived in the stone house across the street. Although he rented the station, he tended to buy his gasoline from his friend, B. R. Foster, in Jonesborough, over 10 miles away.

Ben Fox owned the chicken house at the corner of Main and River Streets, the most popular place in town to slap up a circus poster or to take a photograph. He purchased chickens and eggs from farmers, like many country stores, and every few days would truck them off to market.

The southwest end of Main Street is today comprised of brick storefronts, most of them unoccupied. This store was run at various times as the Huffman Brothers Grocery Store. It was also operated by owners Fred Stanton and Doyle Richardson. Today it houses Richard Donoho's Artistry in Glass.

The train from Knoxville arrives on a winter afternoon during the 1950s. Beside the Southern Railway tracks is the Lone Oak Hotel with double porch and the old Williams Mill behind it.

Four

A Farming Community

Sandra Broyles tries out her pedal car in front of the Lone Oak Hotel. Even before her feet could reach the pedals, this baby was comfortable with seeing tractors and other agricultural implements come through town.

Newton Good feeds his flock. Free-range chickens were the rule up through the 1960s. They were capable of cleaning up bugs around the farm while feeding themselves, except for a little laying ration scattered on the ground. Most country stores accepted chickens or eggs in lieu of cash. With the exception of an occasional fox and the preacher coming to Sunday dinner, free-range chickens were safe until paved roads increased automobile speeds.

Spring plowing on a farm near Limestone exposes the rich soil of Washington and Greene Counties, which has provided sustenance for families since the days of the first settlers. For most of the counties' history, tobacco was king. Nowadays beef cattle holds sway, with tobacco disappearing and dairy declining. Closer to Johnson City, farmland is turned into housing developments, and the new agriculture is landscaping and lawn care.

56

Students at Washington College Academy went on to improve their own dairy herds after raising registered Jersey milking cattle and their calves. From left to right are Willie Holt, Dale Rowe, Don Yeager, and two unidentified.

The late John Henry Price was the only son among Jessie Price's 12 children. T. Claude Hensley photographed John Henry in 1985, and he described the Price family as "fine, hardworking people. Just look at John Henry's hands and you knew he milked a lot of cows."

W. F. Smith bought a trainload of Hereford cattle from Texas in the 1950s and had them shipped to Limestone, where they were unloaded and driven about a mile down State Route 34 to Smith-Dale Farms.

One good thing about being an unincorporated town is that there is no city government to ask permission from if you wish to drive cattle down Main Street. As soon as the cattle were unloaded into Smith's holding pens next to the railroad station and the train cleared the crossing, horsemen were able to start the drive. It was one more aspect of Limestone's Wild West appearance.

John C. Smith and herdsman Everett Miller are pictured with one of Smith's prize bulls, Domino Seth. The Smith-Dale herd was nationally famous and was written up in the *Hereford Breeders Association* magazine.

Farm workers take a break in the shade, but their little girl keeps on playing. Before the days of day care centers, children grew up doing what their parents were doing.

"Bos, here bos!" Ladies betray their rural heritage by engaging in a cattle calling contest while dressed in their fine suits at the Washington County Fair on the Washington College campus during the 1930s.

Livestock judging at the Washington County Fair on the Washington College campus in the 1920s showed cattle, horses, and mules.

Threshing on the U. M. Bradley farm, on Old Heritage Road north of Limestone, was a community affair. The ladies brought out lunch for the workmen. A belt runs to a steam engine off the edge of the photograph to the right. Teams of mules and people obscure the actual threshing machine.

The Washington County Fair was held at Washington College for many years. The school regarded providing a modern agricultural curriculum as its mission and provided self-help scholarships to students, who would tend animals, work in gardens, can produce, and do laundry and ironing. Today the regional Appalachian Fair is held in Gray, north of Johnson City.

61

Thomas A. R. Remine feeds his chickens on the family farm on Remine Road. When emergency 911 service was extended into Washington County in the early 1980s, the county commission was asked to provide consistency in road names. "The name sometimes changes as it passes one prosperous farm to another," the 911 director said. "It's not only prosperity," replied one commissioner. "It's also big families, and they all voted for me."

One way to finance new equipment for the Limestone Volunteer Fire Department was to grow a tobacco allotment and sell it. Shown here grading the tobacco from left to right are (first row) Ray Street, Bob Cutshaw, Tiny Dewall, Dutchie Humphreys, Thurman Hensley, David Cutshaw, Bill Collette, and Archie Jones; (second row) Lyle Broyles, Roy Greene, and Elbert Ayers.

Robert Chandley drives his hand tractor in 1947. New tractors were not available until after World War II, so Bob improvised. He removed the bodywork from a Ford Model A, put oversize wheels and chains on the back, and he was set to plow.

North of town before the coming of the four-lane U.S. Highway 11E was open country and hay fields.

John C. Smith's Sunset Dairy Farm was on Davy Crockett Road south of Limestone. Dewey Mitchell and Hilt Norris hand-milked the registered Holstein herd for 50 years. The barn burned around 2001.

Cutting hay in downtown Limestone makes it clear that this is a rural community.

Five

EDUCATION AND RELIGIOUS LIFE

Welcome School, a two-room country school, stood near the Keebler farm southwest of Limestone. Primary grades were taught in one half of the building, while grades five through eight were taught in the other half. Many people living today received their education in similar schools.

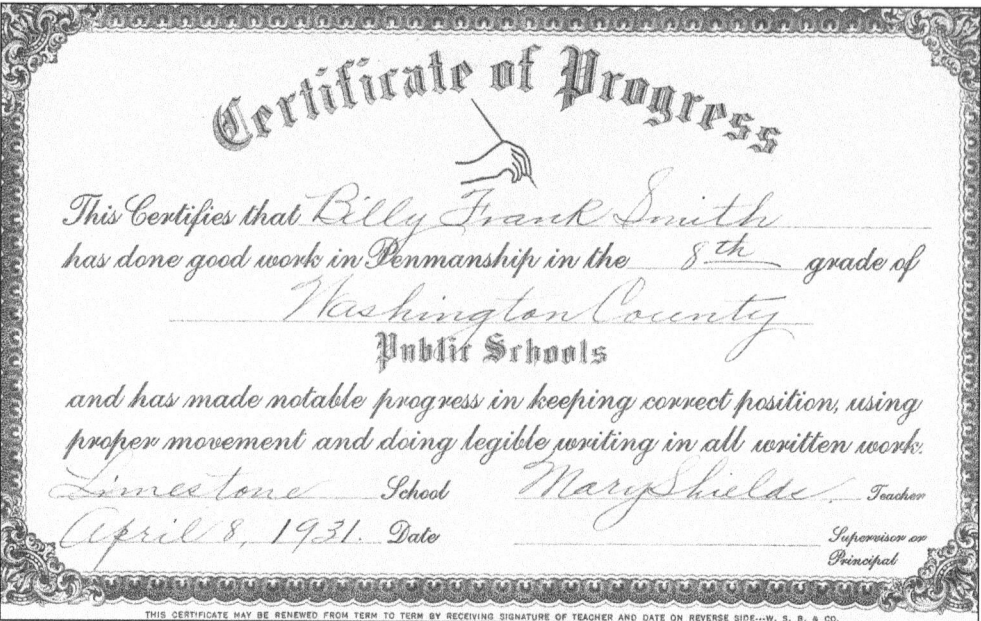

Certificate of Progress

This Certifies that *Billy Frank Smith*

has done good work in Penmanship in the *8th* grade of

Washington County

Public Schools

and has made notable progress in keeping correct position, using

proper movement and doing legible writing in all written work.

Limestone School *Mary Shields* Teacher

April 8, 1931. Date _____ Supervisor or Principal

THIS CERTIFICATE MAY BE RENEWED FROM TERM TO TERM BY RECEIVING SIGNATURE OF TEACHER AND DATE ON REVERSE SIDE—W. S. B. & CO.

A public school eighth-grade handwriting certificate for Billy Frank Smith drew snickers from employees at W. F. Smith Grain, who were accustomed to seeing Smith's signature scrawl. It was usually pointed out that his aunt, Mary Shields, was the teacher.

The class photograph of the old Limestone grammar school required all these children to stand still without blinking.

Students and faculty alike posed annually in front of Limestone's frame grammar school before it burned in 1922.

Girls at Limestone School in 1938, from left to right, were Patsy Stangers, Marie Shelton, Virginia Mathews, Cristine Cartwright, and Louise Humphries.

67

The class of 1934 at Limestone School enjoyed this break in the sunshine.

A class photograph from Limestone School c. 1946–1950 shows, from left to right, (first row) Anna Joyce McCracken, ? Corby, Wayne Holland, ? Vest, Joyce Broyles, Barbara Vest, unidentified, Edna Maude Ruble, Gail Keebler, ? McCall, unidentified, and Sonny Keebler; (second row) unidentified, Virginia McMackin, two unidentified, Joyce Holland, Charlotte Shelton, two unidentified, Jerry Gray, and unidentified. The brick schoolhouse was built in 1922 and torn down in 1989 after consolidation of county schools.

The sixth grade class at Limestone School in 1942–1943 was already looking forward to attending high school at Washington College, a private school that worked with the county on a tuition arrangement before county high schools were built.

The 1949 Limestone basketball team was comprised of, from left to right, (first row) Dick Stanton, Lynn Adams, and Charles Vest; (second row) Tommy Williams, G. W. Hall, Bobby Treadway, Frank Williams, Hubert Showman, Glen Hensley, and Teddy Blankenship. Students who went on to high school attended Washington College, which actually quit offering college degrees in the early 1920s but kept its college charter.

The baseball team at Limestone Grammar School was, from left to right, (first row) Gene Hamblin, Jimmy Fox, Jimmy Treadway, Bruce Landers, Eugene Mitchell, and Marshall Holt; (second row) W. C. Hunt, unidentified, Jim Collette, Raymond Holt, Bobby Moore, Bill Jaynes, and unidentified. Not many small towns could boast of having their local highway patrolman be a man who played in the World Series with Babe Ruth.

Charlie Kate Huffman (left) and her best friend, Mary Blane Fox, are shown at the Limestone School that burned in 1920.

Westview School today is on Old State Route 34 midway between Limestone and Washington College Academy. Population growth in the county has added classrooms to the point that the board of education has decided that future growth will require new school construction.

The Reverend P. Watson was an early pastor of Limestone Methodist Episcopal Church.

The Limestone Methodist Episcopal Church Sunday school class, c. 1940s, squints in the sunshine. Bib overalls were acceptable church wear when they were new and clean.

The Limestone Methodist Episcopal Church complete congregation is shown in 1908. The old frame church could not contain so many parishioners, and discussions were underway that led to the present-day brick edifice.

Salem Presbyterian Church was built in 1894. The impressive brick structure sits in the center of the Washington College Academy campus. Presbyterians were in the forefront of the abolitionist movement before the Civil War. The issue of slavery and the Civil War eventually divided the Presbyterian Church into Presbyterian USA and Cumberland Presbyterian.

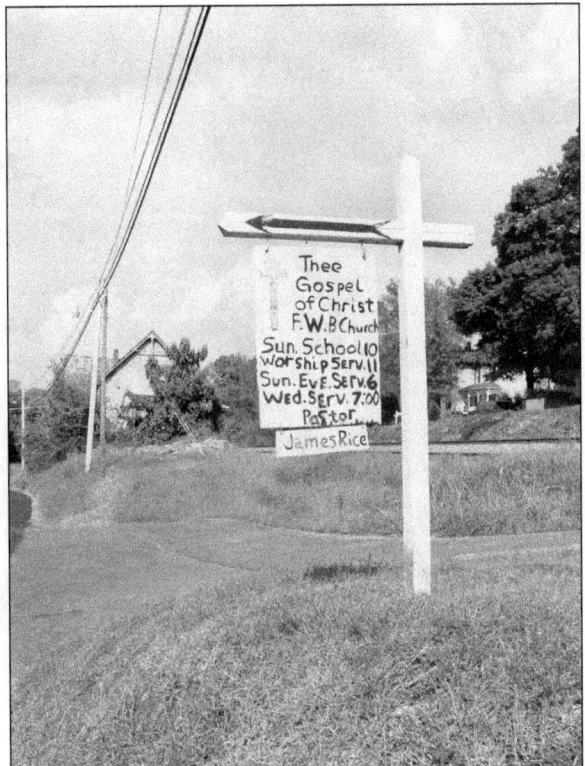

This sign on Main Street directs anyone to the Gospel of Christ Freewill Baptist Church.

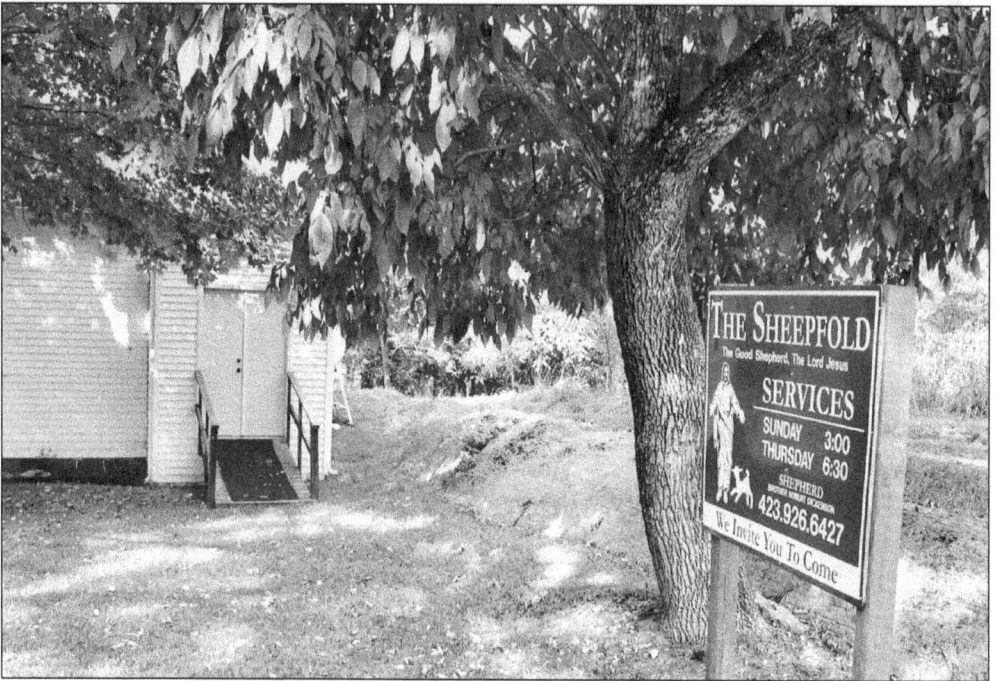

A sign for the Sheepfold, a predominately African American congregation, is next to one of the limestone outcrops that identifies the geology of the community and the bedrock faith of the congregation.

The simple lines of the Sheepfold church bespeak a faith that goes straight to the heart. Most of the African American parishioners live within walking distance.

Six

COMMUNICATION AND TRANSPORTATION

This steam roller was used during the paving of State Route 34 through Limestone. It comes down a hill into town and does a left turn in front of the fire hall, running parallel to downtown on the other side of the railway tracks. At the southwest end of town, it does a right turn under the track in front of the Gillespie stone house. The Esso service station once stood on this corner.

A foreman during the building of Highway 107 along the Nolichucky River south of Limestone looked at his young employee, Wilford Broyles, and said, "You're the boniest boy I ever did see." The nickname "Bones" stuck.

A steel-lugged tractor pulls a road grader in a demonstration at the Washington County Fair at Washington College. Virtually all county roads were mud or gravel in the 1920s, and the annual spring grading to smooth out the ruts was a must.

Limestone's Southern Railway station is a perfect example of railway Gothic architecture. Buying a fare from the station agent brought a passenger going no farther than Jonesborough or Afton a chance to see the train flagged down when the agent flipped the semaphore to stop.

A telegraph key, a regulator clock that displayed the date, lanterns, and a suit and tie were among the necessities required to be the Southern Railway depot agent in Limestone. D. H. Dewald was the last one before the station was closed with the end of passenger service in the early 1950s.

In the late 1940s, the Southern Railway ran its first streamliner through Limestone. Folks would drive to the grade crossings through Washington and Greene Counties to watch it pass.

Teddy Williams Sr. demonstrates in October 1964 how he carried the Limestone mail sack to the curve, where it could be hooked by the passing train as it slowed. Limestone was not a regular passenger stop for the Southern Railway, so the mail was picked up on the fly and incoming mail was tossed out at the Main Street crossing.

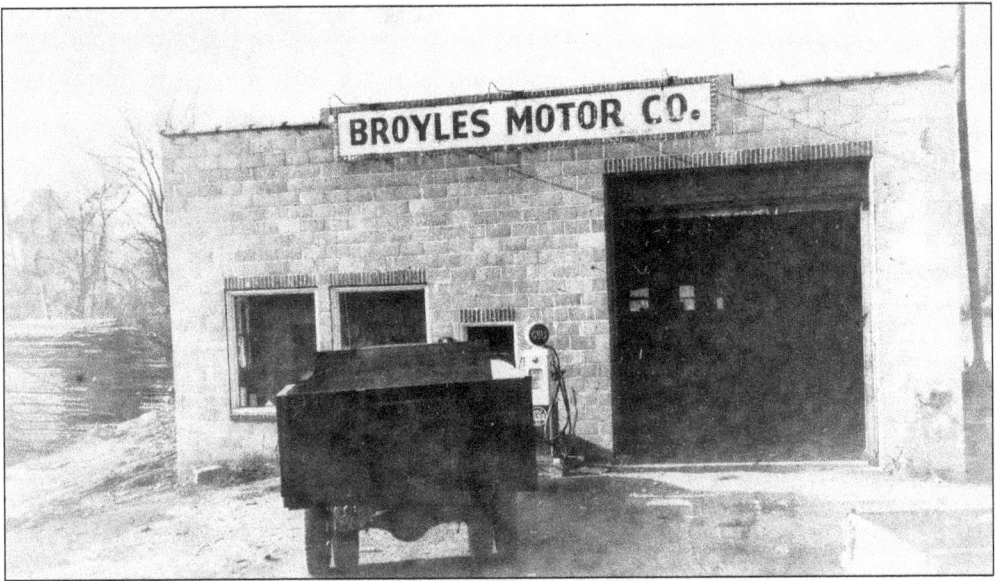

Broyles Motor Company is located at the southwest end of the business district. The Broyles brothers were recognized as mechanical geniuses for anything that needed fixing. Today this building is a shell, with doors and windows gone and with a Ford Thunderbird sitting inside. Wassan Broyles, grandson of his namesake, continues the tradition inside the old Keebler-Smith hardware store, which he bought at auction.

The young Joe Broyles (left) is pictured fooling with Keith Nelson at the East Side Service Station in 1956. The O. C. Arnold Feed Store stands behind the station.

Joe Broyles demonstrates his air cycle. He put a gasoline engine on a tricycle frame that he welded together and mounted a giant propeller on the back. Inspired by the air boats of the Everglades, the fan on the Air Cycle was able to propel Joe down Main Street. Joe tinkered with the air cycle until he died, later adding a propeller shroud. He was working on a child's motorized car when he died. Both machines are still in Wassan Broyles's garage on the site of the former Limestone Motor Company.

A driver's shoulder patch from the old W. F. Smith Trucking Company is part of the family memorabilia owned by W. F.'s daughter, Martha Nell.

Rigs from W. F. Smith Trucking Company load up with hay. Started in the 1930s, W. F. Smith Trucking took in W. F.'s brother and father as partners in 1950, when it became Smith Grain and employed about 250 mechanics and drivers for 100 rigs. Most runs then were done with refrigerated rigs, and a codriver went along to keep the perishables moving. It later became Smith-Dale Farms and was later sold to ValleyDale Farms. It was Limestone's biggest industry.

A fuel delivery to Joe Williams's Esso Station in the 1930s was done with a truck that would be too small for today's fuel consumption levels. Even truck drivers wore bow ties then.

The Rural Searchlight.

LIMESTONE, TENNESSEE, THURSDAY, OCT. 25, 1906.

EPING TAB ON THE WORLD

COMMERCIAL

SOCIOLOGICAL

INDUSTRIAL

Literary Notes.

The November Delineator

Magnolia Flour Metodies

Correspondence.

IOWA.

Limestone Enterprise

LIMESTONE, TENNESSEE, THURSDAY, FEBRUARY 16, 1911.

VY MOVEMENT ACCO MARKETS

iferings on Limestone Very Large and the ·ices Hold Good

ALONG THE RIVER

Items About Big Folks and Big Things in the First Civil District

CLAXTON MAY BE NAMED

Gov. Hooper's Action, Anent Failure of Dyer's Confirmation, Awaited

PRESIDENT TAFT DEFEN RECIPROCITY AGREEM

ITEMS FROM RHEATOWN

A·gues for Protecti Exceeding Difference Cost, and Slight Pr

William F. Piper moved on to publish the *Limestone Enterprise* between 1910 and 1914. This effort carried more local news and was more successful in attracting local advertisements from the likes of Keebler and Miller Hardware; B. E. Brabson Clothing; and Limestone Roller, millers of flour, meal, and feed, J. H. Kirby, proprietor. In the 1920s and 1930s, Limestone went on the air with WGJS, an unlicensed radio station run by G. J. Solomon and Sam Nave, broadcasting from the second floor of Solomon's Hardware until it was closed by the Federal Communications Commission. Those who remember its power output wonder how the feds ever got wind of it.

The *Rural Searchlight* was published Thursdays by W. F. Piper and A. W. Stonesifer for $1 a year between 1905 and 1908. This issue from October 25, 1906, was a mix of poetry, obituaries, and correspondence lifted from other newspapers, leading with a "Keeping Tab on the World" column. In order to sell advertising space, the columns needed to be filled with useful information.

The Victory Buses ran three times a day from Limestone through Bowmantown, Sulphur Springs, and Gray Station to Eastman Chemical and Holston Ordnance defense plants during World War II. With wartime gasoline rationing, a national 30-mile-per-hour speed limit and worker ranks thinned by military service, plant owners bused workmen and women in from all over the three-state area.

The Limestone route for the Victory Bus that ran to Kingsport during World War II went through the villages of Bowmantown and Sulphur Springs three times a day, taking workers to the defense plants in Kingsport, primarily Tennessee Eastman and Holston Ordnance.

This is the entire telephone book for Limestone on February 1, 1911. To place a call, you rang the operator and gave her the name of whom you wanted her to plug into.

LIMESTONE EXCHANGE 2-1-1911

Andrews' Wine of Life Best for Women
Take no Substitute. :: Ask Your Dealer

R. M. MAY & SON WHOLESALE and RETAIL
Domestics, Outings, Underwear, Hosiery, O. N. T. Spool Thread, Blankets, India Linens and Stoneware.
Phone 33 ∴ ∴ Jonesboro, Tenn.

Mountcastle-Phlegar Hardware Co., Inc.
Johnson City, Tenn.
Both Phones, 6
WM. J. OLIVER PLOWS
Hardware, Stoves, Ranges, Paints, Oils, Wall Plaster, Cement, Doors and Windows.

L. Armstrong
G. H. Hartsell
D. A. Hasparger
J. J. Marshall
William McKay
F. R. Martin
J. J. Milburn, M. D.
Charley Cochran
J. M. Miller
J. A. Shanks, Merchant
N. C. Winslow
J. N. Young
Arnold & McCollum, office
Mrs. Fraker
D. F. Hartsell
Thomas Bolton
B. E. Broyles
U. S. Walters
J. A. Bayless
Roller Painter
Mack Broyles
Charley Fox
U. H. Keebler
John Sherict
Mrs. J. B. Pence
E. D. Pence
R. N. Collum
G. W. Cartwright
I. M. Smith
John McCracken
L. C. Adams
L. Armentrout
C. W. Armstrong
D. F. Bolten
D. Armstrong
Mrs. Nan McMackin
C. B. Carson

C. M. McMackin
B. F. Carson
J. W. Keys
R. F. McMackin
J. B. McCrackin
J. A. Squibb
R. McCollum, Dentist
J. B. Moor
F. A. R. Remine
J. B. Crookshank, Merchant
J. M. Mangold
Jake Range
J. B. Bright
J. D. Barkley
S. R. Morlock, M. D.
U. S. Keebler
B. F. Broyles
E. D. Remley
Lois Remine
Keebler & Miller Hardware Co.
Depot
A. B. Bradley
N. M. Bradley
N. C. Remine
N. L. Bradley
A. J. White
O. H. Doyle
Charles Baxter
Keebler & Thomas, Merchants
J. G. Barker
S. E. Dotson
J. M. Good
Mrs. Reames
J. D. Good
W. M. Bright, M. D.
R. O. Huffaker, M. D.

Tucker-Toney Co. ERWIN, TENN.
We handle the Worth Hats,
Best Hats for the Least Money

Ask your grocer or phone us for
Snow Flake Patent Flour   **H. B. STALEY CO.**
It won the Medal at Jamestown for its
Purity and Baking qualities.   MARION, VA.
94

Frank Williams was a Tennessee highway patrolman in Limestone and drove this Chevrolet in 1941. Clarence Tilly Walker, the other state trooper in the area, is remembered for driving a 1935 Chevrolet.

Seven

OVERCOMING ADVERSITY

The iron automobile bridge at the east end of Main Street was almost awash during the July 20, 1921, flood.

The entire town was inundated on July 20, 1921, when heavy rains brought Limestone Creek out of its banks. This photograph, taken from the railway embankment, shows the mill at the west end of Main Street, looking toward the Lone Oak Hotel.

Marshal "Popeye" Holt's milk truck went off the curve on State Route 34 in front of the fire hall and fell onto the Southern Railway tracks. The curve coming into town claimed many a wreck and still does today.

TRAIN WRECK - - 1911 - - EAST LIMESTONE

A train derailment in Limestone turned out everybody in town. Most of the blacks in town once worked on the railroad. In those days, the races were segregated even for a photograph.

A passenger train wreck on State Route 34 west of town in 1918 reportedly left no one injured. Steel cars did not telescope into one another as the old wooden "varnish" did, and passengers could still raise windows to vacate wrecked cars.

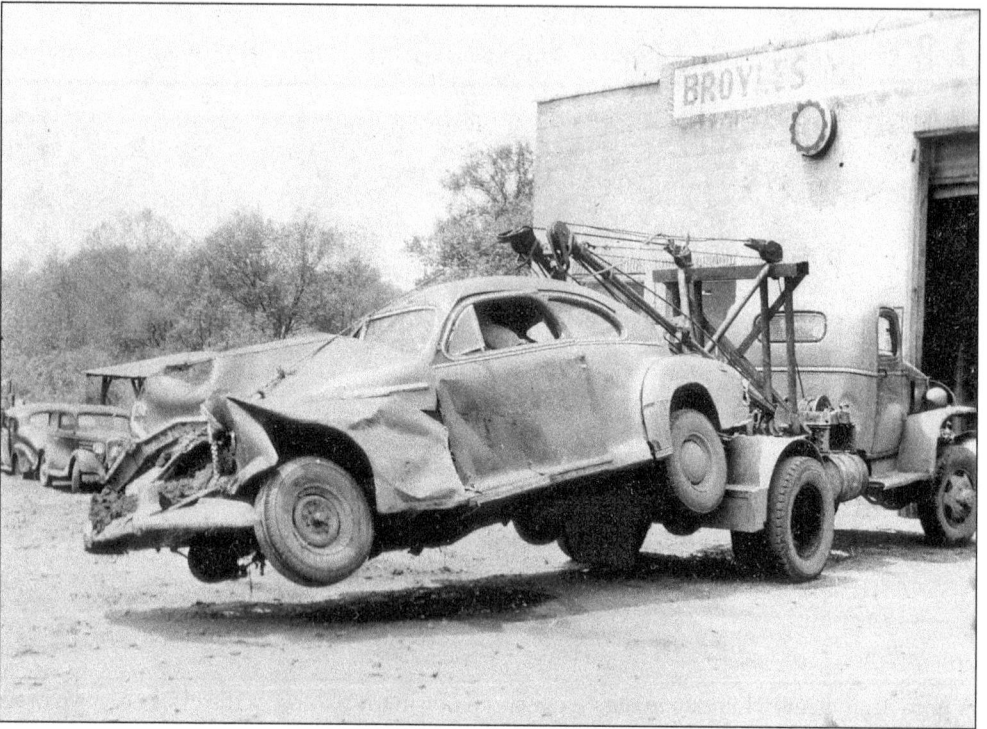

Bringing a wreck into Broyles Garage, which stood beside the Lone Oak Hotel, was a common occurrence. Bones Broyles often drove night wrecker duty and took his four-by-five Speedgraphic camera along so he could sell wreck photographs to the newspapers.

In 1956, Roy "Dutchie" Humphreys saw an advertisement in the *Wall Street Journal* for a 1937 Autocar ladder-pumper fire truck. As head of the Limestone Ruritan's community improvement committee, he knew the nearest fire departments were in Greeneville and Jonesborough, both 15 miles away. The club sent Dutchie, Marion Lee Broyles, John A. Matthews, and Paul Estepp to buy the truck. The 750-gallon-per-minute pumper included 250 feet of hose and a 50-foot extension ladder. They bought it for $3,800, drove home on May 2, 1957, and, after some sleep, gave a demonstration at Jockey Creek, using only one 50-foot section of hose.

On Saturday, May 17, 1957, the call came that downtown buildings were on fire. Due to bad hose threadings on the town's newly arrived 1937 Autocar fire truck, there were only three usable sections. It was not long enough to bring water from Limestone Creek. Jonesborough was called but took a long time to arrive with its Jeep pumper and tank trailer. Greeneville wouldn't come unless $250 was paid. Harvey Usary put up the money when the wind switched and blew toward his service station near the end of the bridge.

Everyone in town stood on the railroad embankment on the other side of Main Street to watch the fire being fought. When Jonesborough arrived, enough hose was borrowed to put Limestone's new truck in service from the creek. Greeneville arrived and laid a line to the creek but blew the packing out of their pump. They didn't charge anything and asked if they could hook onto the Autocar. The fire put an end to Limestone's Main Street of wooden buildings after the southwest end of town burned in August 1939.

Two buildings were lost completely in the 1957 fire. Bill Garrison's Barber Shop is the single-story building, formerly the U.S. Post Office. The two-story Odd Fellows Hall had an upholstery shop downstairs. The Milhorn Building had the second story fall into the first and was also almost totally lost. The men of Limestone pumped water for six hours. An apartment building and an abandoned service station are all that is left of this end of Main Street today.

The 1957 downtown fire was fought from behind Main Street as the water had to be pumped from Limestone Creek. Here men are watering down the buildings saved during the fire. At left is the burned-out roof of the Milhorn Building.

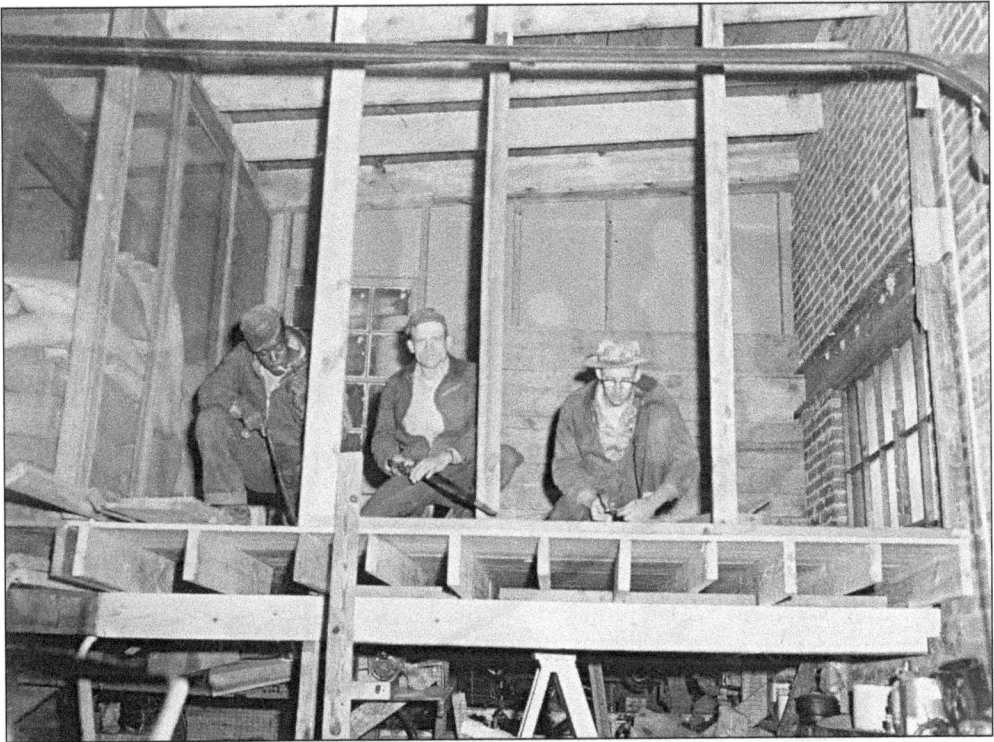

The Limestone schoolhouse was leased to the Ruritan as a clubhouse after consolidation. They voted to convert it into a fire station. From left to right, John Gillespie, Beck Estepp, and Dutchie Humphries are at work with their framing hammers.

In this early photograph of the Limestone Volunteer Fire Department, taken in the mid-1960s, the trucks are the original 1937 Autocar with its tank increased to 500 gallons, a Reo tanker for country use, and a Dodge. Firemen from left to right are Clarence Eads, Bill Collette, Tom Jaynes, Joe Jaynes, Roy "Dutchie" Humphries, Beck Estepp, Fred Bailey, Thurman Hensley, Milton Hensley, James Brown, Roy Greene, and Jack Jeffers. Eads went on to become chief of the Johnson City Fire Department.

The Limestone Volunteer Fire Department was formed on May 6, 1957. Gordon "Buck" Conway was elected chief, with Everett Miller as his assistant. Both were Smith Grain employees, and W. F. Smith offered his building as fire hall and telephone number 2660 to receive fire calls. Someone worked there 24 hours a day. Two fire halls and several trucks later, the firemen, from left to right, were (first row) Vaughn Baldwin, Ronnie Reed, David Cutshaw, Jeff Williams, and Randy Bailey; (second row) Thurman Hensley, Joe Jaynes, Sam Showman, James Mahafey, and George Jaynes, who is currently mayor of Washington County.

LIMESTONE VOLUNTEER FIRE DEPARTMENT

PHONE	DAY	NIGHT
FIRE CALL	2711	2660
Everett Miller	2660	3563
John Anderson	3561	3561
M. L. Broyles	2933	3583
Jo Jaynes	——	——
Beck Esteep	2874	2874
Milton Hensley	——	3502

When you call be sure to give clearly your name and the location of the fire.

"Help Us To Help You"

CALL IN TIME

Before 911, call cards for the Limestone Volunteer Fire Department were distributed to all residents of Limestone. In the late 1950s, one only needed to dial four digits. It quickly became apparent that a single number was needed that could blow the whistle.

Eight

SPARE TIME

Hanging out at the East Side station in the 1950s, the discussion was probably about that Davy Crockett movie and how there was probably money to be made from it if the world only knew Crockett was born in Limestone. The philosophers, from left to right, are Dale Broyles (partially obscured), Floyd Collette, Cubby McCracken, George Jaynes (the future mayor of Washington County), Claude Hensley, Gary Broyles, Robbie McCracken, Gene Nelson, Claude Martin, and unidentified.

When it was within its banks, Limestone Creek was a delightful picnic spot, but a lady had to be prepared to look away just in case those boys were swimming "nekid" under the railroad bridge.

The flood plain in downtown Limestone is a natural ball field in dry weather. Racial integration was a fact of life in small towns where neither blacks nor whites had enough players to put together a baseball team. They could either play with each other or against each other.

Buford Williams, Charlie Williams, and Hershel Barlow are pictured at the loafer's bench on the southwest end of Main Street in 1956. The masonry buildings replaced the wooden buildings that burned in 1939. After this photograph was taken in 1957, the wooden buildings on the northwest end of the block burned.

In 1958, Charlie Williams (standing) and Billy Hensley (seated) were photographed by T. Claude Hensley at the East Side Service Station, the former W. F. Smith garage.

Gilford "Bones" Broyles is shown here on his first "skeeter," a truck chassis stripped to the bare bones. He was the photographer for most of the Limestone photographs of the 1930s and 1940s, and he saved many of the earlier John Laws photographs.

The west end Esso station was in ruins before it was torn down. It was located across from the Gillespie stone house. This was the site of the Civil War Battle of Limestone Station. On September 8, 1863, the 100th Regiment Ohio Volunteer Infantry met 1,000–1,500 Confederates led by Gen. Alfred E. "Mudwall" Jackson of Jonesborough and fought until they ran out of ammunition. About 250 surrendered and spent the remainder of the war in Confederate prisons. Losses in the three-to-five-hour battle were 85 men. A makeshift hospital was set up on this site. (Courtesy of T. Claude Hensley.)

Nine

WASHINGTON COLLEGE

Washington College was founded by
the Reverend Samuel Doak in 1780,
the year he sent the Overmountain
Men off with a ringing sermon from
Sycamore Shoals in Elizabethton to
engage the British at the Battle of
King's Mountain, the turning point
in the Revolutionary War.
He also founded Tusculum College
in Greeneville.

The Washington College Post Office opened in 1897. Shown here from left to right are Clinton Bowman, two unidentified, postmaster and merchant Nathaniel Taylor Bowman (with rifle), clerk John Stone, clerk O. H. Reeser, Elizabeth Bowman, Mrs. N. T. Bowman, Frank Bowman, and Lettie Bowman. N. T. Bowman later served as a magistrate on the Washington County Court and as county tax assessor.

The 1908–1909 Washington College baseball team included, from left to right, ? Kyll, pitcher and right field; Charles Vail, second base; E. J. Adams, third base; ? Houston, shortstop; ? Dillow, catcher; ? Mitchell, right field; ? Greenway, center field; Clarence Tilly Walker, pitcher and right field; ? Bowman, first base; unidentified, mascot; ? Kelley, field; and ? Smith, field. This is the earliest known photograph of major-league standout Clarence E. "Tilly" Walker.

The Washington College baseball team is pictured 1909–1910. Tilly Walker is in the center of the first row. "Nobody loved kids like Tilly," said Johnny Mitchell. "He was forever taking them to games or buying them overalls or shoes. He got me into professional ball as a shortstop with the Greeneville Burleys."

The 1916 Washington College women's basketball team played in skirts and middies. They are, from left to right, (first row) Mary Kate Copp, forward; Ilene Greenway, guard and forward; and Mary Lou Alexander, forward; (second row) Elizabeth Bowman, manager, guard, and center; Velma Carson, guard; Bill Stanton, coach; and Ella Kate Self, center.

Tilly Walker went straight from Washington College to the Washington Senators in 1911. Three new faces on the Washington College team from Bridgeport, Connecticut, appear to be older than college age. From left to right are (first row) C. D. Bowman, pitcher and center field; James Rochimati, first base, Bridgeport, Connecticut; E. J. Adams, third base; W. S. Mitchell, left field; and J. S. Solen, second base, Bridgeport, Connecticut; (second row) Jack Strickfus, shortstop, Bridgeport, Connecticut; A. W. Bright; F. L. Greenway, pitcher, center field; and J. H. Dillow, catcher; (third row) B. N. Kelley, pitcher; J. C. Rittler, owner; and B. G. Robeson, right field.

Clinton Bowman enjoyed hunting on the family farm near Washington College with Bell, his thoroughbred bird dog and her son, Bob. He grew up on the campus as son of the Washington College postmaster and went on to become a Presbyterian minister.

Clint Bowman served in France with the American Expeditionary Force during World War I. He went on to become a clergyman and served the First Presbyterian Church of East St. Louis, Illinois, until his death in 1953. He was one of many distinguished graduates of Washington College, which includes six U.S. congressmen, many judges and clergymen, and many Washington County officials.

Carnegie Hall at Washington College is shown before Temple Hall was added. It was the administration building and a classroom building. Washington College Academy held its last commencement in 2001. Although the campus continues to be shut down, GED classes have been held in the president's residence, and a reopening is planned for 2007.

Temple Hall's auditorium, being finished here, was an addition to Carnegie Hall that included an auditorium and a downstairs basketball court that terrified visiting teams. A balcony around the court provided spectator viewing but was so low that visiting players were in danger of bumping their heads. Using this home court advantage, Washington College players attempted to utilize a defense that pushed their opponents to the edge.

While Washington College has attracted students from around the world, it has always best served the rural residents of Washington County, most of whom were day students. In the early days of the automobile, before there were paved streets on campus or paved roads in the county, parents simply drove their Model Ts across the campus lawn to pick up their children at the end of the day.

Girls at Washington College worked in the laundry doing their own washing and ironing. For many years, contributing to the school through manual labor was a part of the school policy.

Harris Hall, girls' dormitory at Washington College, later had a dining hall added to the right side of the building. Built in 1842, it is the oldest building on campus. During the Civil War, Union soldiers occupied the upper stories and stabled their horses on the ground floor. It burned in 1911, and the farm was mortgaged to pay for the rebuilding.

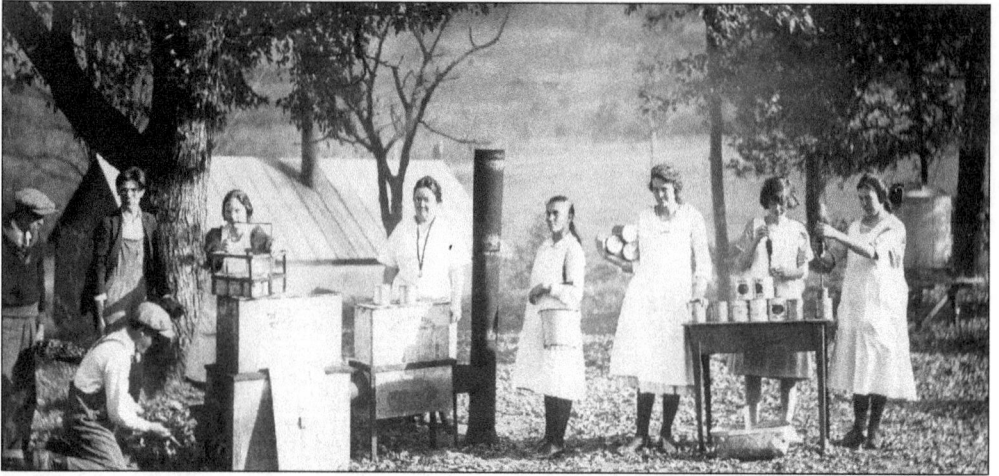

Washington College self-help students are canning tomatoes from the school farm. Most food produced by students became part of the school menu.

An overall view of the Washington College campus shows Salem Presbyterian Church (left), Carnegie Hall (center), and Harris Hall (right). Later additions included a boys' dormitory, primary education building, and the Harris gym.

The beautiful baby contest at the Washington County Fair during the 1920s judged babies to determine the best, although the same standards were not used for livestock judging.

A Boy Scout encampment at Washington College was probably part of the Washington County Fair, annually conducted on campus in the early 20th century.

The Bowman house at Washington College was the home of postmaster N. T. Bowman and his children, Clinton and Elizabeth, who also graduated from the school.

The boys' dormitory at Washington College was a frame structure that burned in the 1950s.

On January 10, 1954, the boy's dormitory at Washington College caught on fire and burned down to the foundation. The realization is just beginning to sink in to the boys on the sidewalk that they have lost everything.

Fortunately everyone escaped without injury from the boys' dormitory at the height of the 1954 fire.

Some of the boys displaced by the 1954 dormitory fire were from a distance and were taken in by the Reverend and Mrs. R. R. Gilbert. From left to right are Richard Donoho, Asheville, North Carolina; Mrs. Gilbert (playing the piano); Gilbert and his daughter, Allyson; Ramon Casteanass, Cuba; Henry Alvarez, Puerto Rico; Eduardo Nadarse, Cuba; and Grace Blankenship, Flag Pond, a regular resident at the Gilbert home. Donoho today runs Artistry in Glass with his wife in Limestone. He was the first emergency medical technician with the Limestone First Responder Squad in 1986.

Mullins Hall, a brick structure, replaced the boys' dormitory lost to fire. Present at the dedication were, from left to right, Luke Warrick, Jimmy Taylor, unidentified, Dean Alexander from East Tennessee State University, Washington College Academy president Henry Jablonski, mathematics teacher Pop Mullins, the dorm's namesake, and three unidentified.

Carrie Warrick (third row, off to the far right) led the music department at both the school and Salem Church. This is the 1927 college glee club. It was the same year she married Luther M. Warrick. An accomplished pianist, she performed worldwide and demanded the same dedication from her students that she used in her own practice. Her booklet setting forth her principles is still in use. She was considered stern by many, but anyone with the courage to return her steely gaze would see a twinkle in her eye. She continued to be active in the music department at the church until the day of her death at the age of 98.

A watermelon feast at Washington College included, from left to right, Mrs. N. T. Bowman, N. T. Bowman, Mildred Bowman, Ray Ruble, and Dr. Roy Henry Ruble. Dr. Ruble practiced in Limestone until after World War II and, at that time, was one of three doctors in the community. Today, since the closing of the Limestone Medical Clinic, residents must drive or be transported to Johnson City or Greeneville.

An on-campus crew built the Scott House on the Washington College campus. The photograph indicated that it included N. J. Bowman (left), Will J. Cannon (center), and Clinton Bowman (right). The house was originally built for Mrs. Willoughby, according to a notation on the photograph.

Students entering the campus for the first time are confronted with the Salem Presbyterian Church cemetery as soon as they turn off of State Route 34. It created vivid, although false, first impressions on the nature of discipline on campus.

Washington College dairy students got hands-on experience, as shown by the milking buckets, milk cans, and manure rake they hold. The school's dairy herd was comprised of registered Jerseys and Guernseys, as the high butterfat content of these cattle led to a greater variety of potential dairy products than a Holstein herd.

The Washington College barns included a demonstration barn (left), built by the McCormick Reaper Company of Chicago. The large dairy barn is still standing. It was later upgraded to a milking parlor, but only its tile walls remain.

Roger Dillow (left) and Keith Guinn show their registered Hampshire sheep. Dillow went on to a distinguished career in the army where he was a helicopter pilot; today he lives in retirement in Jonesborough where he twice ran unsuccessfully for mayor.

Ramsey (left) and Bobby Jack Williams pose with registered Guernsey calves in front of the Washington College truck usually driven by Ralph Armentrout, who was the person who held things on campus together for years as farm manager and general campus "fixit" man.

The janitor for the Salem Presbyterian Church was known only as Bill, was said to be from way back in the Cumberland Mountains, and was a fixture on campus for many years.

The boy's junior varsity basketball team at Washington College wore Future Farmers of America T-shirts in the 1950s. In 1905, the school dedicated itself to the need to instruct in modern agricultural methods. The self-help program allowed local children the chance to enroll. In 1923, the school focused attention on high-school students, although it retained its college charter.

Planning for the Harris Gymnasium, the newest building at Washington College, was conducted by, from left to right, Pres. T. Henry Jablonski, science and Spanish teacher Mary R. Campbell, business teacher Travis Smith, and coach John Maxey. Jablonski resigned as president in 1980, the school's bicentennial.

These men are building the Alan Harris Gymnasium in 1971 at Washington College Academy. The new facility included not only a gym, but a swimming pool and classrooms. The swimming pool was later destroyed in a gas explosion in 1996. After the county opened David Crockett High School and Washington College became a true private school, it acquired academy status.

Pres. T. Henry Jablonski is shown with Washington College foreign students during a graduation ceremony in the early 1950s. The presence of black foreign students on campus just as the U.S. Supreme Court ordered desegregation of Southern schools in 1954's *Brown v. Board of Education* put white students at ease in an integrated setting that was almost unique in the South.

The Washington College senior class trip to Washington, D.C., was an annual event for students and faculty. This was the 1953 group.

Washington College students get down, but in true rural fashion, it's a square dance rather than rock and roll. This scene from the early 1950s saw Jane Matthews at the microphone as the caller. She later became the only librarian Westview School has ever known.

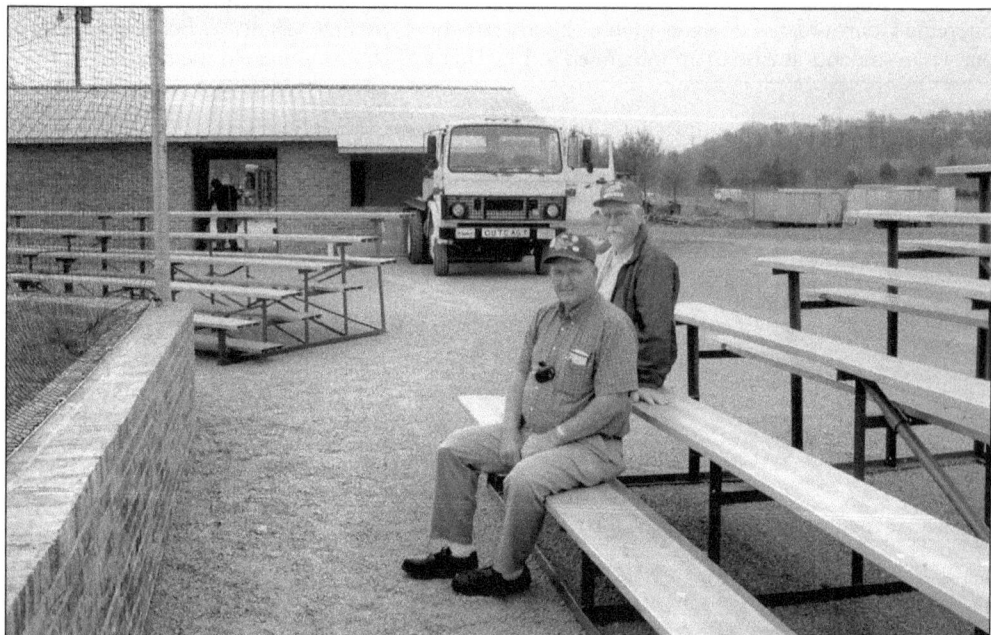

The Washington College Ruritan, founded in 1969, has saved Washington County taxpayers over $500,000 in landfill tipping fees by recycling trash at the convenience center they opened in 1986. The sale of recycled trash has built their clubhouse, baseball field, and concessions stand. Shown before the baseball field dedication are Pres. Larry Waddle (left) and Jack Campbell, past president.

116

Ten

BROYLESVILLE

Broylesville is pictured from the hill above town during the 1970s. From left to right are the Broyles Mercantile Establishment, the 1797 inn, and the cobbler's house.

Built in the 1830s by Adam Broyles, son of one of the community's founders, the Broylesville Mercantile Establishment is a mix of Greek Revival and Federal styles. Broyles was a blacksmith, merchant, innkeeper, and farmer. Local legend says the grated basement windows indicate slaves were kept there while awaiting auction.

The road not taken was the one that led into Broylesville. Once bypassed by the railroad in the 1840s, the town gradually withered. At its peak, there were tanneries, blacksmith shops, a cooperage, foundry, distillery, sawmill, and shoe factory. Barrels of flour and whiskey were put on rafts in the creek and floated to Knoxville via the Nolichucky River, where everything was sold. At its peak, between 200 and 300 families lived in the community.

Home from college, two Washington College students in their letter sweaters put their agricultural training to the test in a field alongside Gravel Hill Road in Broylesville. This photograph was taken in the 1920s.

The Bashor mill in Broylesville brought its water in a flume. Later it was converted to a turbine mill, with water flowing through the foundation directly into the turbine. A distillery once stood on the other side of Little Limestone Creek.

The 1912 Parker house in Broylesville features a hipped roof and a porch on all four sides. It was once the home of miller James Taylor. Current owners are the Reverend Garland and Jean Thayer.

The cobbler's house in Broylesville, c. 1840–1850, is currently unoccupied and was one of several industries in the town. It is located at the ford of Little Limestone Creek. Inside scroll saw work on the stair risers is in the shape of boots.

The c. 1812 Ira Green–McQueen house in Broylesville is pictured. It featured a concrete foundation and two interior chimneys with a fireplace in every room. Kyle and Louise McQueen have owned it since 1947.

Adam Broyles's wife, Rosanna, purchased a house at the Little Limestone ford in 1797 and extended it into an inn. Presidents James K. Polk, Andrew Jackson, and Andrew Johnson stayed here at one time or another. Slaves were sold on a stone in front between 1803 and 1809 and intermittently into the 1830s but not often enough for it to be considered a slave market.

This was how the Bashor-Taylor mill looked when it was first purchased by Margaret Gregg in 1994. It was first purchased by Erline Ledford, who learned it was about to be dismantled for lumber.

Multimedia artist Margaret Gregg came to Tennessee from Chicago. Her works range from quilts and fabric constructions to metal sculpture. She has lived and set up her studio in the mill since she first bought it. There were some cold winters at first.

The waters rose to the doorstep at Margaret Gregg's mill in Broylesville during the flood of August 4, 2000, when 10 inches of rain fell.

Debris from the flood of August 4, 2000, surrounded the Taylor mill in Broylesville. Soon a crew of friends and volunteers arrived with chain saws and cleaned up the debris. Today flowers bloom in Margaret's peace garden.

Significant reconstruction was required to bring back the mill. Here Gerald Price (left) and Junior Newell engage in a major corner rebuilding project on the foundation.

Serious foundation work followed the flood in the summer of 2000 as Harold Edwards's crew replaces the sills with termite-resistant hemlock.

The Thanksgiving arts and crafts sale at Mill 'N Creek Gallery saw Theresa Marlowe showing her work in 1997.

November 2001 saw the new metal roof in place, the final step in exterior restoration. Further work inside has provided more usable living and studio space, and outside work has included a retaining wall along the creek and steps down to the water. Too often the history of the Limestone area has been a recounting of what has been destroyed. The Bashor-Taylor-Gregg mill is the one conspicuous exception.

State Route 34 was a dirt road with Gravel Hill Road cutting to the left to the Bashor Mill in Broylesville when this photograph was taken. It makes the bend around the Parker House as the traveler in his Model T Ford returning from Washington College and headed for Limestone shouts over the wind to his companion, "There's Broylesville. We're already half-way home."

127

www.arcadiapublishing.com

MAP SEARCH

Discover books about the town where you grew up, the cities where your friends and families live, the town where your parents met, or even that retirement spot you've been dreaming about. Our Web site provides history lovers with exclusive deals, advanced notification about new titles, e-mail alerts of author events, and much more.

MADE IN THE USA

Arcadia Publishing, the leading local history publisher in the United States, is committed to making history accessible and meaningful through publishing books that celebrate and preserve the heritage of America's people and places. Consistent with our mission to preserve history on a local level, this book was printed in South Carolina on American-made paper and manufactured entirely in the United States.

This book carries the accredited Forest Stewardship Council (FSC) label and is printed on 100 percent FSC-certified paper. Products carrying the FSC label are independently certified to assure consumers that they come from forests that are managed to meet the social, economic, and ecological needs of present and future generations.

FSC
Mixed Sources
Product group from well-managed forests and other controlled sources

Cert no. SW-COC-001530
www.fsc.org
© 1996 Forest Stewardship Council

Find Your Place in History.